HISTORIC

COMMUNITIES

The General Store

Bobbie Kalman

Crabtree Publishing Company

COMMUNITIES

Created by Bobbie Kalman

For Noreen and Charlie Parsons,
my favorite storekeepers

Editor-in-Chief
Bobbie Kalman

Research
Julie Read

Writing team
Bobbie Kalman
Niki Walker

Managing editor
Lynda Hale

Editors
Niki Walker
Virginia Mainprize
Greg Nickles
Petrina Gentile

Computer design
Lynda Hale

Special thanks to
Doon Heritage Crossroads, St. Augustine's Oldest Store Museum, The Toy and Miniature Museum of Kansas City, Lang Pioneer Village, MTRCA (Black Creek Pioneer Village), Upper Canada Village, Kathleen Stocking and the New York State Historical Association, Genesee Country Museum, Old Sturbridge Village, Judie Ellis, and Marion "Toby" Tyler

Separations and film
Dot 'n Line Image Inc.

Printer
Worzalla Publishing Company

Crabtree Publishing Company

350 Fifth Avenue	360 York Road, RR 4	73 Lime Walk
Suite 3308	Niagara-on-the-Lake	Headington
New York	Ontario, Canada	Oxford OX3 7AD
N.Y. 10118	L0S 1J0	United Kingdom

Cataloging in Publication Data
Kalman, Bobbie, 1947-
  The general store

(Historic communities series)
Includes index.
ISBN 0-86505-432-0 (library bound) ISBN 0-86505-462-2 (pbk.)
This book examines features of nineteenth-century general stores, including merchandise, packaging, communications, and the post office. It also looks at the barter system, the store's place in community life, and the role of the storekeeper.

1. General stores - Juvenile literature. I. Title.
II. Series: Kalman, Bobbie, 1947-   . Historic communities.

HF5429.K3 1996   j381'.1   LC 96-26737
                                               CIP

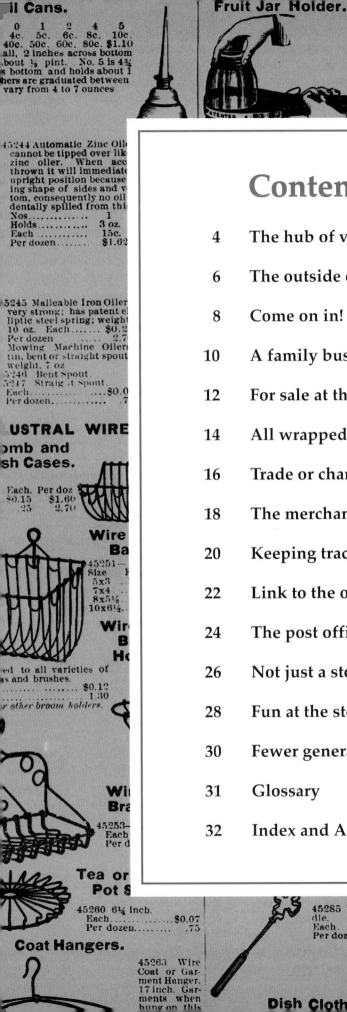

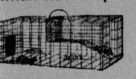

Contents

The hub of village life

The post office was located at the general store. This storekeeper has just sorted the mail, which was delivered by stagecoach.

Before there was a general store in an area, life was very difficult for farmers and other settlers. They had to grow their own food, make their own clothing, and carve household items from wood. When a store opened, farmers could trade their vegetables, eggs, butter, and crafts for things they could not make or grow, such as metal tools, lamp oil, and sugar. The store also provided small communities with exciting new goods and services such as newspapers from the city, canned foods, postal service, and items from around the world.

Helping communities grow

The store helped a community grow by attracting settlers to the area. Tradespeople such as printers, blacksmiths, cabinetmakers, and potters soon joined the growing community. They set up workshops near the general store, creating a main street. The community eventually became a town with homes, a schoolhouse, and church. At the center of it all was the general store.

A gathering place

The general store not only attracted people to the community, it also helped create a neighborly feeling among them. People who did not see one another in their day-to-day lives often had a chance to chat at the general store. It was a place for farmers and townspeople to discuss weather and crops and exchange local gossip.

(above) Great conversations took place over a game of checkers. These two players also got plenty of advice about which move to make next! (below) The store's porch was another popular place for customers to chat and pass the time.

5

The outside of the store

Early general stores were simple two-story buildings. Many were not even painted. Most stores had two large display windows— one on either side of the front door. Women's items were displayed in one window and men's in the other. A porch roof or canvas awning prevented the sun from fading displays and offered customers a shady spot to rest. Wooden sidewalks, called **boardwalks**, ran along the front of many stores.

Putting up a front

Storekeepers wanted people to notice their store. To make it appear taller than the other buildings on the main street, some merchants attached a **facade**, or false front, to the top of their store. A storefront facade is a wall that has nothing behind it. False storefronts were common in frontier towns of the west. Square false fronts, called **boomtown fronts**, were especially popular. The expression "to put up a good front" is often used today. What do you think it means?

Come on in!

A small brass bell tinkled as customers pushed open the door. Stepping inside, shoppers noticed an unusual blend of smells that included spices, leather, coffee, and kerosene.

Drawers and bins

Long wooden counters stretched along both sides of the store. The drawers and bins built into them held spices, ground sugar, coffee, flour, and seeds. The glass cases sitting on the countertop displayed expensive items such as pens, perfumes, jewelry, and silverware. Behind the counters, shelves covered the walls from floor to ceiling. They were stocked with pots, pans, dishes, bolts of material, bottled medicines, and countless other goods.

(top) Hundreds of items are sold at this store. The clothing department is at one end, where a mannequin models long johns and a top hat. (bottom) This woman is asking for a closer look at the silverware that is locked in the display case.

Organizing the goods

Although the store was crammed with goods, it was not difficult for customers to find the items they wanted. Everything was grouped in special areas called **departments**. Tools were hung in the hardware department. Ready-made clothes were displayed near the boots and shoes, and bolts of fabric sold by the yard were stacked in the yard-goods section. Sacks and barrels of flour, sugar, molasses, and vinegar were found beside the meat counter in the grocery department.

A place for paperwork

The merchant's office was tucked in a corner at the back of the store. It contained a wooden filing cabinet and a small desk for bookkeeping. Sometimes the merchant built shelves and cubbyholes for sorting his papers.

(above) The merchant had a small office area for doing his bookkeeping.
(below) This customer weaves her own wool fabric but buys cotton at the store.

A family business

The general store was usually a family business run by a man, his wife, and their children. Although the wife helped with the store, only the husband was called the storekeeper or merchant. A man was considered to be the head of the family, so he was also thought of as the head of the business.

Teamwork

Running a store was plenty of work! Six days a week, the store opened early in the morning and closed late at night. Both the merchant and his wife worked long hours. They served customers and stocked shelves all day long. When the merchant was busy unloading goods or traveling to pick up supplies, his wife looked after the store.

The children's chores

Children did chores before and after school and all day Saturday, the busiest day of the week. Sweeping, unloading wagons, polishing brass, grinding coffee and sugar, weighing items, and wrapping purchases were just a few of their jobs. The children also learned how to keep accounts.

Hired help

Often there was so much to do that the merchant had to hire a clerk. Most clerks were young men whose families did not have a farm on which they could work. Some clerks lived above the store and worked in exchange for their room and meals. Others lived elsewhere and were paid a wage. Storekeepers gave their clerks many rules to follow. For example, they were not allowed to smoke or attend dances.

Clerks worked thirteen hours a day and were given only one evening off. They had to attend Sunday School or church each week and give part of their wages to the church.

opposite page (top) The storekeeper's daughter has lots of chores, including dusting and sweeping. (bottom) Storekeepers and their families often lived in rooms behind the store. This baby just woke from her nap. She is curious about the young customer in the store.

11

For sale at the store

Hand-dipped candles were part of the stock at the general store.

The general store carried a variety of goods, or **merchandise**. Some of these goods were grown or made by people in the area, and others came from far away. The main types of goods sold at the general store were **produce**, **groceries**, **dry goods**, **housewares**, and **hardware**. The merchant always tried to keep these items **in stock**, or available for sale at the store.

Produce

Farm goods such as fruits, vegetables, eggs, meat, and grains are called produce. In the past, furs and lumber were also part of the produce department. Most of the produce sold in the general store was bought from nearby farms. People also brought homemade goods such as bread, pies, jams, and jellies to trade with the storekeeper.

Grocery items

Grocery items included such foods as spices, tea, and sugar. Later, canned goods were also part of the grocery department. Many groceries were **imported**, or brought from outside the community. The storekeeper bought goods from nearby cities and other countries. Before railroads connected cities and towns, it was expensive to ship goods from place to place.

Once railroads were built, it was faster and cheaper to transport goods. Trains moved large amounts of groceries and stopped in small towns to drop off deliveries for general stores. Groceries that were once luxuries became cheaper when transported by train, and people started buying them regularly.

Clothing, tools, and dishes

Dry goods included cloth, thread, ribbon, and ready-made clothing. Metal tools and gadgets were called hardware, and dishes, brooms, and mops were known as housewares. Besides these types of goods, the store sold hundreds of other items, including seeds, books, and medicines.

Special orders

Sometimes a customer wanted an item that was not found in the store, such as a fancy hat, a mechanical toy, or a pocket watch. The store-keeper either ordered the item from a catalog or purchased it during his next trip to the city.

Mrs. Hale is picking up a very special item. She has waited several weeks for this hat, which was ordered from a catalog. She is choosing ribbon and silk flowers to trim the new bonnet.

All wrapped up

In the past, groceries were displayed and sold differently than they are today. Paper bags and cardboard boxes had not been invented yet, so most foods were packaged in wooden barrels or cloth sacks. Customers often supplied their own containers for taking purchases home from the store. Breakable goods such as eggs were carried in baskets. Molasses, vinegar, and honey were taken home in clay pots and jars.

Pick a poke

Cloth sacks were expensive, so the merchant saved them for packaging large amounts of weighed goods. He wrapped small purchases in paper. He tore a piece of paper from a roll, shaped it into a cone with one hand, and poured the goods into it with the other. This package was called a **poke**.

(above) Some goods were sold by weight. The merchant measured the amount a customer wanted and poured the purchase into a cloth bag. (below) Many grocery items, such as crackers, were shipped in barrels.

Buying in bulk

In the early 1800s, cloth sacks and wooden barrels were used to ship food items in large quantities, or **bulk**. Settlers who lived far from the store often bought staples such as flour and oatmeal in bulk. They wanted these foods to last so they would not have to make the long trip to the store more than once a month.

Bulk containers

Storekeepers used a variety of crates, sacks, and casks to store and display their goods. The following bulk containers could be found at a general store:

Crates are wooden packing cases. Their sizes vary according to what is packed inside.

Bales are bundles of goods that have been squeezed together, wrapped in cloth, and tightly tied or stitched.

Gunny sacks are large bags used for holding a variety of bulk goods, such as produce, sugar, and spices. Sacks are made from a coarse cloth called **burlap**, which is woven from the fiber of the jute plant.

Bags are similar to sacks, but they are smaller and usually made of cotton.

What are casks?

A **cask** is any type of container made with wooden staves. The following are all casks:

A **barrel** is a large cask that has curved wooden sides and a flat top and bottom. It holds between 117 and 160 liters (31 and 42 gallons) of liquid.

A **kilderkin** is a cask that holds half as much liquid as a barrel.

A **tierce** can hold one-and-a-half times the liquid that a barrel can contain.

A **hogshead** is a large cask that is equal to two barrels.

A **keg** is a strong, small barrel. A **drum** is a straight-sided keg used for storing fruit or fish.

A **firkin** is a small wooden barrel that holds butter, lard, or soap.

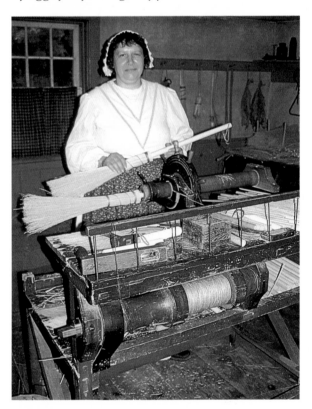

Today Mrs. Hale is bartering a basket
of eggs for packages of flower seeds.

Trade or charge?

Most settlers were farmers who did not earn wages working on their farms. They had very little money, but they had valuable crops and livestock that could be traded for other goods. At the store, farmers exchanged their produce for items such as cotton and silk, leather saddles, and metal tools. **Bartering**, **store credit**, and **charging** were three methods of trading at the general store.

The barter system

Before general stores were established, farmers bartered, or traded, among themselves. It was often difficult to barter because one farmer had to want what another was offering for trade. The merchant made bartering easier because he took produce in exchange for goods sold in his store. Farmers traded crops and homemade goods for items that they could not get from other farmers.

Store credit

Sometimes the farmers' produce was worth more than the goods the farmers took from the store. They received store credit to make up the difference. Since most of their earnings were spent at the store, the farmers preferred to use the credit system instead of cash, which could be lost or stolen. Each time a farmer made a purchase, the storekeeper subtracted the value of the purchase from the total credit in the farmer's account.

Craftspeople could trade their wares directly with farmers. They could also use their goods to barter at the general store. This broom maker often takes several brooms to the store and accepts store credit in exchange. She can use the credit to buy various store items at a later time.

Charge it!

Farmers often spent all the credit earned from one harvest before their next crops were ready. Without crops or money, they had nothing to trade. They could still make purchases, however. The storekeeper knew that the farmers would have produce to trade within the year, so he allowed them to charge purchases to their account. The farmers owed the merchant money and promised to repay the debt when their crops were harvested.

Farmer Friesen is bringing the merchant a barrel of sauerkraut to pay for some of the goods he charged over the winter. In his record book, the merchant subtracts the value of the sauerkraut from the amount Farmer Friesen owes him.

The merchant goes shopping

Once or twice each year, a country storekeeper went to a big city on a buying trip. He looked for items that were not made or grown in his small community. The merchant spent weeks comparing the goods offered for sale by various **wholesalers**. Wholesalers are companies that sell products made by several **manufacturers**. The storekeeper hoped to buy enough merchandise to stock his store until the next trip.

The royal treatment

In the city there were so many companies selling goods that they competed for the storekeeper's business. Some sent him railway tickets, and some paid for his hotel and meals. Others took him to plays and concerts.

What to buy?

It was difficult for the storekeeper to know how much merchandise to buy for his store. Sometimes he was left with bare shelves before his next trip to the city and, at other times, he had too much stock and was forced to put it on sale.

The storekeeper's first task was to purchase goods, such as shoes and farm equipment, which were always in stock at the store. He also bought items specially requested by his customers, such as books, dresses, and fine cloth. Sometimes he took a chance on buying products he thought his customers might like, including the latest toys, household gadgets, and jewelry.

Stirring up excitement

The storekeeper's return from a buying trip was an exciting event in the community. Customers couldn't wait to see the new merchandise and hear the latest news from the city. The merchant often placed an ad in the local paper to list the goods he purchased and inform customers that their special orders were ready to be picked up. He also hung signs in the store windows to advertise the brand-name items he was selling.

The storekeeper hopes a wealthy farmer will buy this fancy dollhouse. If not, the merchant might have to put it on sale or keep it for his own children.

The villagers are excited to read about the new products that are available at the store. Their special orders have also arrived!

Keeping track of trading

It was important for the storekeeper to keep track of everything he bought, sold, or traded. By keeping records of who owed him money and to whom he owed money, the merchant knew if his store was earning a profit.

The merchant did not want customers to know how much profit he made on his merchandise. In the early days, he used a code to mark both the cost and selling price on every item in the store. He made up code words that had ten different letters and then gave each letter a number from zero to nine. Each merchant used different words to make the codes difficult to break.

Wolf tracks in my red wagon!

For example, one store might have used the letters in "wolf tracks." Wolf stood for the numbers 1234, and tracks represented 567890. Another storekeeper might have chosen "my red wagon" as a code for 12 345 67890.

If "wolf tracks" was the code, a pair of boots would have been marked WOO/WRS. The boots cost the merchant WOO, or $1.22, and the selling price was WRS, or $1.60. To make a profitable trade, the merchant had to barter the boots for an item with a value greater than $1.60. If "my red wagon" was the code, how much would items marked MOW, RAD, and YEN have cost? The answers are on the left.

The storekeeper is making up a code to fool his customers. Will they guess the buying and selling prices of his goods anyway?

```
W O L F    T R A C K S
1 2 3 4    5 6 7 8 9 0

M Y   R E D   W A G O N
1 2   3 4 5   6 7 8 9 0
```

Answers:

1. MOW = $1.96
2. RAD = $3.75
3. YEN = $2.40

Using money

How confusing this system must have been!
By the 1870s, money had become more common,
and people bartered less often. They simply
bought and sold goods. Since more people
paid cash for their purchases, a modern form
of pricing that used numbers rather than code
letters was introduced. Storekeepers began
using cash registers to tally purchases and
hold money.

A better method of bookkeeping

The merchant began keeping books in which
he wrote the cost and selling price of everything
in the store. He also wrote down every item he
bought and sold. This new bookkeeping system
allowed the merchant to see exactly how much
money he was making or losing.

*The cash system made a storekeeper's
life much easier. Cash registers
totaled the value of a customer's
purchases in dollars and cents.
The merchant did far less bartering.*

Link to the outside world

The sign posted at this store announces that a livestock auction will take place soon.

The general store served as the communication center of the town. People went to the store not just for supplies but also to hear or pass on the latest news and gossip. In later days, they could also make telephone calls at the store.

Community connection

The townspeople stopped to chat on the store's porch or around the potbellied stove. They read the notices that were posted on the walls or posts announcing community events and town meetings. When people heard that a neighbor's child was ill or that a barn had burned down, they often posted a sign asking the community for help. Customers helped rebuild the barn or gave money towards the doctor's bills.

Spreading the news

Local news reached the store quickly. If an event was especially exciting, such as the birth of a baby, people sent a note to the store immediately. They knew they could rely on the storekeeper to spread the news. Customers looked forward to hearing the town's latest gossip during their weekly shopping trip.

The storekeeper also informed customers of news he had heard while traveling to other towns and cities. He brought back information on the latest farming methods, fashions, and inventions.

Newspapers from the city

Although some towns had a local newspaper, it often had only a few pages and contained little news from outside the town. Newspapers from big cities provided small towns with a link to the rest of the country. In most towns, the storekeeper was the only person who subscribed to a city newspaper. He kept his copy of the paper in the store for his customers to read.

Telephones

Telephones appeared around 1880, but they were so expensive that most towns had only one. The phone was located in the general store so everyone could use it. Some merchants offered free use of the phone, but others charged a fee for making calls. People did not make or receive calls often, so when they did, the whole town heard about it.

The merchant cannot wait to tell Mrs. Jordan about Mrs. Langdon's new baby.

This settler comes to the store to read about events in other parts of the country.

The post office

Early post offices were located in the general store. Each family in the community had a cubbyhole for receiving letters and packages. When mail arrived, the storekeeper sorted it and put it into the cubbyholes.

Moving the mail

Before railroads were built, mail was delivered by stagecoach. This method of delivery was slow and expensive. Letters coming from a great distance took months to arrive! Stagecoach robberies occurred often, so many people never received their mail.

It was cheaper and faster to send mail once there were trains. If there was a train station in town, mail arrived at the general store every day. Letters sent from far away reached their destination in weeks rather than months.

Mailing and receiving letters

To mail a letter, the sender took it to the general store. There were no envelopes, so the storekeeper folded the letter and sealed it with warm wax. He then pressed the wax with a metal stamp that showed from which town the letter was sent.

Postal tricks

In the 1800s, the person who received a letter paid the postage instead of the person who sent it. If a letter was not opened, the receiver did not have to pay, so some people wrote coded messages on the outside of their letters. The receiver simply read the message and handed the unopened letter back to the storekeeper without paying the postage.

Not just a storekeeper

The merchant in an early town had several roles. Long before the town had a banker, lawyer, or innkeeper, the merchant helped the community by being all these things to the people in the area.

The go-between

The merchant often arranged business meetings between people who did not know one another. For example, when a farmer needed a team of horses to plow his fields but did not know who rented horses, he spoke with the storekeeper. Since the merchant knew almost everyone in town, he knew who had horses to rent. The storekeeper arranged for the two people to meet at the store and charged them a small fee for his service.

The town banker

The few banks that were built in North America in the early 1800s were located in the cities. In small towns, the general storekeeper was the banker. When people had extra money, they sometimes gave it to the storekeeper for safekeeping. The merchant paid these people a small fee, or **interest**, and then used their money to offer loans to other townspeople. The borrowers repaid the loans, with interest, to the storekeeper.

The town lawyer

The storekeeper usually knew more about laws than anyone else and often played the role of the town lawyer. He advised people on deals, helped them make contracts, and acted as a witness when these contracts were signed. Storekeepers also issued marriage licenses.

The town doctor has brought some money to the storekeeper for safekeeping. The merchant has figured out how much interest the doctor should earn for his money and asks him to double-check the arithmetic.

opposite page (top) In some towns the storekeeper even played the role of the dentist!
(bottom) When there were no inns in a town or village, the storekeeper offered travelers food, drinks, and a place to sleep.

Fun at the store

Luke and Amanda loved going to the store with their parents. The family shopped on Saturday, when the children were not in school. This week's trip was especially exciting because Mother and Father promised to buy the children candy as a reward for doing all their chores.

Mother and Father planned the trip carefully. They made a list of items the family needed and loaded their wagon with vegetables, cheese, butter, eggs, buns, and homemade jellies. They would trade these goods for the items they wanted.

Checkers and advice

After unloading the wagon, Father warmed himself by the potbellied stove. He played a game of checkers with the town doctor and asked for advice about the aches and pains in his back.

Cotton and candy

Mother looked at bright cottons in the yard-goods section while Amanda and Luke headed for the jars filled with expensive, mouth-watering candies. They couldn't wait to get their tasty reward!

Fewer general stores

Many old general stores, such as the two on this page, have been converted into gift shops, workshops, or restaurants.

The railway brought the general storekeeper more goods at lower prices, but it brought competition as well. In the late 1800s, mail-order companies used the railroad to send catalogs and goods to people in small towns. These companies offered the latest goods at lower prices than those at the general store. The railroad also made it possible for people to travel to the cities or other towns to purchase anything they needed.

Specialty shops and department stores opened in many small towns, taking business away from the store. Banks and door-to-door mail delivery also contributed to the closing of many general stores. Still, general stores have remained popular in some small towns because they continue to offer old-fashioned, friendly service.

Glossary

account A record of finances or business deals

awning A rooflike cloth shelter that projects over a door or window

barter To trade goods for other goods without using money

boardwalk A sidewalk made of wooden boards

bolt A large roll of cloth

bookkeeping The work of recording business deals and accounts; a system for keeping these records

bulk Describes goods that are packaged or sold in large quantities

charge To promise to pay for goods or services at a later date

communication The transfer of any type of information

credit An amount owed to a customer that is kept on record by the storekeeper and used instead of cash

cubbyhole A small compartment

department An area of a store in which similar types of goods are grouped

dry goods Items such as cloth, thread, and ribbon, also known as "soft goods"

go-between A person who makes arrangements between people

groceries Foods other than fresh farm products

hardware Metal tools and utensils

housewares Tools and gadgets that are used in homemaking such as pots, pans, kitchen utensils, and brooms

imported Describes something that was brought from outside the community

in stock Describes goods that are on hand for sale in a store

interest A fee for borrowing money

livestock Farm animals such as cows, horses, and sheep that are raised for home use or profit

manufacturer A company that makes goods, often with the use of machines

merchandise Goods that are for sale

merchant A person who buys and sells goods; a person who owns a store

postage A charge for transporting mail

potbellied stove A short, rounded, wood-burning stove

produce Farm products such as fruits and vegetables

"put up a good front" This expression can mean "to pretend to be something you are not." It can also mean "to act as though everything is well when it is not."

special order Describes an item that is ordered by a storekeeper at the request of a customer

stagecoach A horse-drawn coach that transported people, mail, and baggage

staple A basic food or other product that is needed and used often

stave A long, narrow strip of wood that forms part of the sides of a barrel

stock (*noun*) The goods sold at a store (*verb*) To refill shelves and cases with goods for sale

wage Payment for work or services

wholesaler A company that sells goods to storekeepers

yard goods Cloth that is sold by length

Index

Acknowledgments

Photographs and reproductions
Thomas Neill/Old Sturbridge Village:
     pages 13, 14 (both), 16 (top), 23 (bottom), 27
Marc Crabtree/Montgomery's Inn: page 12
Marc Crabtree/Genesee Country Museum: cover
Doon Heritage Crossroads, Region of Waterloo:
     pages 5 (bottom), 11, 21
Bobbie Kalman and Peter Crabtree: pages 4, 6, 7,
     10, 16 (bottom), 20, 30 (both)
Jim Bryant/Upper Canada Village:
     pages 22, 23 (top)
Metropolitan Toronto and Region Conservation
     Authority: pages 8 (bottom), 9, 17,
     19 (bottom), 26 (bottom)

National Archives, C1115: page 5 (top)
New York State Historical Association:
     pages 24-25
St. Augustine's Oldest Store Museum:
     pages 8 (top), 26 (top)
Toy and Miniature Museum of Kansas City:
     page 19 (top)

Illustrations and colorizations
Barbara Bedell: cover, title page, pages 6-7,
     9, 18 (both), 28-29
Antoinette DeBiasi: page 13
Rob MacGregor: page 10

WESTERNSCHOOL